What's for lunch?

oranges

© 1999 Franklin Watts
96 Leonard Street
London
EC2A 4RH

Franklin Watts Australia
14 Mars Road
Lane Cove
NSW 2066

ISBN 0 7496 3338 7

Dewey Decimal Classification Number 634

A CIP Catalogue record for this book is available from
the British Library

Editor: Samantha Armstrong
Series Designer: Kirstie Billingham
Designer: Jason Anscomb
Consultant: Dr Philip Ashurst
Reading Consultant: Prue Goodwin, Reading and Language
Information Centre, Reading.

Printed in Hong Kong

What's for lunch?

oranges

Claire Llewellyn

W
FRANKLIN WATTS
NEW YORK • LONDON • SYDNEY

Today we are having oranges for lunch.

Oranges are a **fruit.**

They contain **vitamins,**

minerals and **fibre.**

They help us to stay healthy.

Oranges grow on trees
in hot countries, such as Brazil,
where the weather never gets very cold.
Farmers grow the trees
in **orchards** or **groves.**
Plenty of space is left between the trees
to give them room to grow.

Each new orange tree
grows from an older orange tree,
called a **rootstock.**
The farmer makes a little cut
on the rootstock, and then slides a branch
with a new **bud** on it into the hole.
After about eight weeks,
the bud starts to grow.
The farmer cuts off every other branch
and the new orange tree grows
from the sprouting bud.

In spring white flowers called **blossom**
grow on the orange trees.
After the flower petals drop off,
the fruits start to swell.
At first they are small and green.
By the autumn they have grown larger,
and in late autumn they begin to turn orange.

Farmers leave the oranges on the trees
for one or two months.
Before **harvesting,** they test the juice
to make sure it is sweet.
The oranges are then picked by hand.
They are picked very carefully
to avoid damaging the skin.
Then the oranges are taken to a packing house.

At the packing house,
the oranges are washed to remove any dirt.
Washing removes the natural **wax**
on the skin of the oranges.
The oranges are re-waxed by a machine.
Wax makes the oranges look shiny,
and helps to keep them juicy.

Next the oranges are **graded.**
The best ones are kept for eating.
They are packed into bags or boxes
and delivered to shops,
markets and supermarkets.

Other oranges are used to make juice.
Machines squeeze out the juice and
remove any **pips**.
The juice is put into
bottles and cartons
and delivered
to shops.

Some juice is treated in a different way.
The water in the juice is removed,
leaving a thick syrup
called **concentrate**.

The concentrate is **frozen**
and taken by ships and trucks
to different countries around the world.
When it arrives, it is allowed to thaw.
Then water is added to it to turn it
back into orange juice.

Orange juice is added to
iced lollies and drinks
to give them a fresh orange taste.

Oranges are used in many different ways.

Orange skin is called **peel.**

Orange peel is full of **oil**.

Orange oil is used to flavour chocolate.

It also adds an orange taste to other food,
such as this orange and carrot cake.

You can eat oranges just as they are
or you can squeeze them
to make your own juice.

Oranges are juicy and delicious,
and help to keep you fit and healthy.

Glossary

blossom   the flowers of fruit trees

bud   the new shoot growing on a branch

concentrate   juice that has had most of its water removed

fibre   something found in some foods that helps us digest what we eat

frozen   when something is so cold it turns to ice. Frozen food stays fresh

fruit   the part of a plant that contains the seeds. Fruit is often sweet and juicy

graded   sorted into different sizes

groves   the fields where orange trees are grown

to harvest   to gather in the crop

oil	the liquid in the skin of an orange
orchard	a field where fruit trees are grown
minerals	materials found in rocks and also in our food. Minerals help us to stay healthy
peel	the skin of an orange. Orange peel contains oil, which is used to flavour foods
pips	the seeds of a fruit
rootstock	the older tree which is used to grow new trees. It is called a rootstock because it has very strong roots
vitamins	things found in foods which keep us healthy
wax	the natural shiny coating on an orange, or a lemon

Index

The author would like to thank Jim Saunt for his generous help and advice in the preparation of this book.
Picture credits: By kind permission of Citrosuco, Brazil: 18, 21, 22, 23; Holt Studios International: 8 (Nigel Cattlin), 11, 13 (Inga Spence), 14, 17 (Nigel Cattlin); Hutchison Picture Library 7 (J. Henderson); P.Millard: 25. Steve Shott cover, backcover; All other photographs Tim Ridley, Wells Street Studios, London. **With thanks to Charlotte Trundley, Alex Wright and Aiken Senior.**